'cause i wanted to know

Poems and Illustrations by
Aaron Cheney

Dream Garden

Renton, Washington

Cover art and illustrations by Aaron Cheney.
Edited by S. C. Moore.

2nd Edition, Published 2016, Dream Garden Publications, an imprint of Gazebo Gardens Publishing, LLC.
www.GazeboGardensPublishing.com

ISBN: 978-1-938281-01-3   (paperback)
ISBN: 978-1-938281-16-7   (e-book)

Library of Congress Control Number: 2016954481

Printed in the United States of America.

Dedicated to my children,
Jeff and Jess.

I Tried

I once tried to see what a telescope sees
when it looks at the mountain on Mars;
so I looked without luck 'til my eyeballs got stuck,
and now I can only see stars.

I once tried to hear what an Indian hears
when he puts his ear next to the ground;
so I listened 'til veins beat like drums on my brain,
and now all I hear is that sound.

I once tried to know what the wisest monk knows
at the peak of a hill in Tibet;
so I studied in school 'til my memory got full,
and now all I learn I forget.

I once tried to taste what a hummingbird tastes
when he puts his tongue into a flower;
but my tongue wouldn't fit so I got mad and quit,
and now all my candy tastes sour.

Don't tell me I'm silly for trying such things,
I tried 'cause I wanted to know,
and knowing means trying and not just relying
on somebody else's say-so!

Bikes, Trikes, Yikes!

If a bike has two wheels,
and a trike then has three,
by simple mathematics,
it seems plain to me,
the next logical step,
is a fork would have four,
so I tried to ride one,
and boy, am I sore!

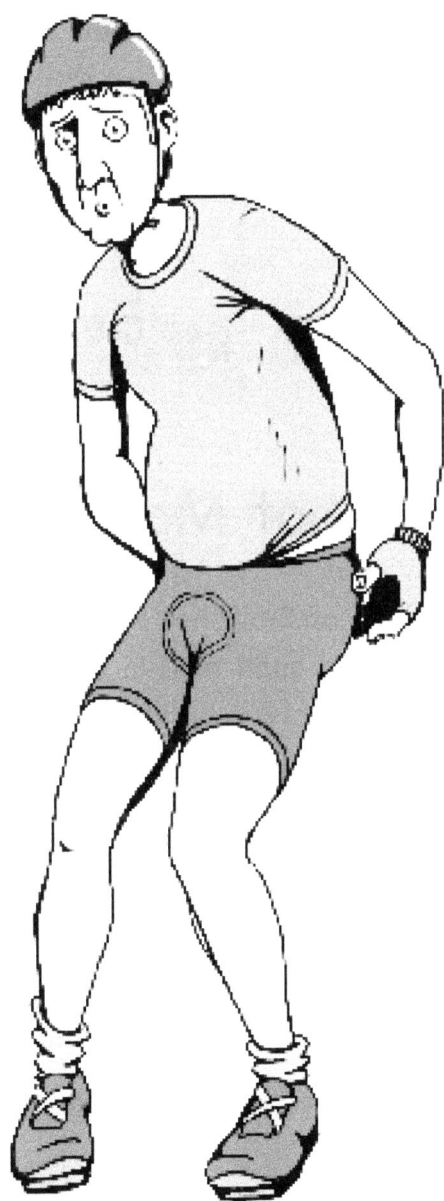

WANTED

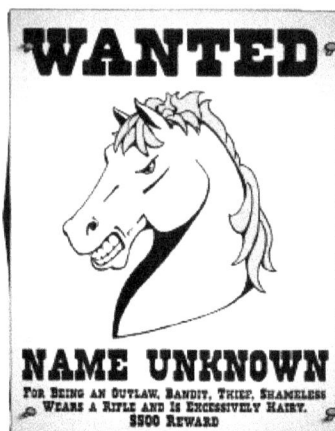

BUCKSHOT MALONE

FOR BEING AN OUTLAW, BANDIT, THIEF, SHAMELESS
WEARS A GUN, AND IS EXCESSIVELY HAIRY.
$500 REWARD

WANTED

NAME UNKNOWN

FOR BEING AN OUTLAW, BANDIT, THIEF, SHAMELESS
WEARS A RIFLE AND IS EXCESSIVELY HAIRY.
$500 REWARD

Buckshot Malone

This is the story of Buckshot Malone
and his horse (who shall remain nameless).
Malone was an outlaw, a bandit, a thief;
in short he was wicked and shameless.

He carried a knife, had a scar by one eye,
and a pistol belt full of hot lead.
Even his horse (name withheld) wore a rifle,
(at least that's what everyone said).

All of his teeth were more crooked
        than straight,
And his sinister grin was ferocious.

His mustache was greasy, his manner uncouth,
and his personal hygiene atrocious!

The hair on his chest was as thick as a rug,
from some potent elixir he'd carry.
And as for his horse,
      (who shall remain nameless),
it was also excessively hairy.

Now this horse (name withheld)
      it was said to breathe fire,
and its eyes were as black as the night.
With heartbeats like thunder
      and hoofbeats like lightning,
just seeing it filled you with fright.

And now we'll commence
      with this sinister tale,
'twas a night dark as any you'll find.
Malone seized the reigns
      and cried to his horse,
"Hya, Daisy!"

...Oh dang!

Never mind.

Freeway to Mars

If I were to build a freeway to Mars,
it would take lots of concrete and big steel bars.
I'd have to have cranes that would fly out in space,
and build spacesuits for almost the whole human race.

Then I'd put them to work building girders and spans,
and hooking up I-beams and mapping out plans,
and whatever else the construction demands.

We could put in an off-ramp direct to the moon,
and a sign as you leave that says,
        "Come back real soon!"
And a billboard about every ten-thousandth mile,
and a rest stop to stop at and rest for a while.

There would be some delays, 'cause there usually are,
and it would cost more than all other bridges by far.
But can you imagine the view from your car?

There wouldn't be stoplights or big intersections,
or slowdowns at intergalactic connections.
We'd all drive as fast as our engines would go,
(unless you were old, in which case you'd drive slow).

But there is one small thing that my plan kind of lacks,
there's no gas station there, so we couldn't get back.
I guess we had all better pack extra snacks!

Gizmo

Of all the super-heroes,
Gizmo is my favorite one,
with his anti-matter gun
and his infra-X-ray eyes,
and his golden wing-tipped helmet
with reflectors in the back,
and the nitro-rocket pack
that he uses when he flies.

He has a boomeranging lasso
and explosive super-gel,
and a super sense of smell
that lets him move without a trace,
and a turbo-hover pod
that goes eight zillion miles an hour,
and runs on solar power
when he flies around in space.

He's very well accessorized
with all the bells and whistles,
like a super-car with missiles
and robotic arms that shoot,
and underwater goggles
with a scope for deep-sea tracking.
I guess the only thing he's lacking
is a super-hero suit!

My Glasses

When I was little, I got my Mom worried.
I told her the things that I saw were all blurry.
So off to the doctor we went the next day,
and got me some glasses.

They sit on my face just under my hair,
and over my nose...right where I stare.
I wear them whenever I'm looking at things,
which is just about every day of my life.

You wouldn't believe what these glasses have seen,
dewdrops and rainbows and blossoms in spring,
and twenty-five yo-yos all tied to one string,
are a few of the things my glasses have seen.

And once as I lay fast asleep on my bed,
while my glasses were sitting three feet
from my head,
they watched as the morning sun crept
in my room,
and battled to closet the darkness and gloom.

I wouldn't have known 'bout this wonderful show,
(I was completely asleep when it happened,
you know),
except for my glasses, who while I lay snoring,
watched it and told me first thing
the next morning.

Stuff

Hacksaw, scissors, pliers, ruler,
rivets, wrenches, hammer, nail.

Seashell, water, swimsuit, ocean,
castle, seaweed, shovel, pail.

Apple, eggplant, kumquat, carrot,
lettuce, peanut, grapefruit, orange.

Linen, button, muslin, cotton,
needle, thimble, thread, and...

And...

My Code

I hab a code,
I hab a code,
Ibe bisruble today.
I hab a code,
I hab a code,
I habit buch to say.

The Lonely Crayon

Of all the crayons in my box,
there's one I never use.
I'm convinced that he is certainly
the loneliest of hues.

I try him out from time to time,
but always put him back.
His pencil point's without a doubt
the sharpest in the pack.

It's not that he's unable
to behave just like the rest.
It's just that he's a little bit
uninteresting, I guess.

'Cause when I try to use him,
he will never leave a mark,
unless the tip is really dirty,
or the paper's really dark.

I didn't want to use his name,
but just 'tween you and me,
I colored this entire page
with him so you could see.

5 Minutes to Bedtime

"How does an airplane fly?"
    'It goes really fast
    and floats in the sky.'

"Why are stars out only at night?"
    'They only shine down
    when the light is just right.'

"Why are gramp's teeth in a jar?"
    'So when he needs them
    he knows where they are.'

"Why do our insides stay in?"
    'Cause they're all glued together
    and covered with skin.'

"What makes a satellite go?"
    'I have to be honest,
    I really don't know.'

"Why are your eyes so droopy and red?"
    'Because I'm so sleepy,
    now just go to bed!'

Yours or Mine?

Is that your hearing aid I hear?
That really high-pitched whine?
'Cause if it ain't your hearing aid,
well, then perhaps it's mine!

Is that your baby parakeet
perched high up in that tree?
'Cause if it don't belong to you,
it might belong to me!

Are these your last two sentences
hanging in the air?
Well, if you didn't say them,
I might have put them there.

Are those my silly rhymes
still rolling 'round your brain?
Well, someday when you're done
with them,
I want them back again.

Suddenly, I Turned Around

by Jeff and Aaron Cheney

Suddenly I turned around
and everything was upside-down!
Airplanes flew beneath my feet
and people dangled from the street.

Pineapple upside-down cake
was right side up,
and everyone's drinks
fell out of their cups.
Kids on swings swung up to the ground
and dragged their feet
on the sky to slow down.

Though I really hate to trouble you,
all the M's turned into W's.
It really was raining cats and dogs,
and mice, and tools, and rocks, and logs...

And beds, and sinks, and cars, and plants,
and rocks, and trees, and underpants.
The more I watch, the more it pours —
I guess I'd better go indoors.

I AM BIG

by Jessica and Aaron Cheney

Suddenly I turn around
and I am big.
I accidentally step on a pig.
All the sunflowers are like twigs.

All the people are like ants.
I outgrew my little pants.
All the houses are so small.
I step over a wall,
because I am so tall.

My head is in the clouds.
I am in a parade with the crowds.
I am so big I can carry cars.
And I am so big I can put my head
in the stars.

Since I am so big today,
I am going to outer space to play.

Three Thieves' Tale

Three terrible two-timing thieves,
trod their tainted trail.
'Til triumphs turned to tragedy,
this trifle tells their tale.

They'd taken treasure town to town,
through treachery, through treason.
Then the treasure triggered tensions,
'tween this thieving threesome.

They took the treasure to their trove,
the tirade that they threw!
'Til tempers turned to tomahawks,
the thieves then totaled two.

The twosome traded taunts,
their thuggish talk too tough to tame.
Then tightened twine to throat,
ticked the tragic tally twain.

The third thief took to tomb,
tripping through the trio's trap.
Then the townsfolk trolled the tract,
the treasure trove they tapped.

The Tale of
the First Jolly Roger

Squinty-eyed Jack was a pirate,
who didn't like pirate type things.
He didn't like broadswords or plundering freight,
and he didn't like parrots or pieces-of-eight.

He didn't like pistols or cannons,
and he didn't like following maps.
He didn't have any tattoos or a scar,
and he never said "shiver me timbers"
or "aaarrrr!"

His shipmates all thought he was wimpy,
the captain just thought he was weird.
When dinner was done they would
drink rum and fight,
but Jack would sneak straight off
to bed every night.

For secretly Jack liked to sew,
he also could knit and crochet.
His runners and doilies were some of the best;
he once knit the captain a brown sweater-vest.

Now this captain was Bilgewater Bob,
the fearsome-est man on the sea,
reputed to be a cantankerous cuss,
both louder and meaner than his blunderbuss.

With his patch and his hook and his peg leg,
he used words like "avast" and "ahoy,"
and while all the deckhands were hoisting the sails,
he paced the deck cracking his cat-o'-nine-tails.

But Bilgewater was in a spot,
pursued by a whole naval fleet,
for looting an English built ship of the line,
and stealing her cargo of jewels and wine.

He didn't know what he should do;
for once in his life he was scared.
His crew and his ship were
outclassed and outgunned,
outwitted, out-sailed, outmanned, and out-runned.

Then Squinty-eyed Jack had a thought,
a thought that grew into a plan!
He flexed all his digits so limber and nimble,
and went to work weaving his needle and thimble.

He sewed like a demon possessed;
he stitched like the wind through the trees.
When both hands were busy
he sewed with his nose,
until there was thread from his head to his toes.

He embroidered some crossbones in white,
with a head-bone above, over black.
And when this new banner was raised and unfurled,
all of the naval fleet's toenails curled.

And right then they gave up the chase,
and turned hard astern and a-port.
Content to let Bilgewater give them the slip,
for none would come near him
with death on his ship.

Then Squinty-eyed Jack was a hero,
his shipmates gave up a great cheer!
From then on they thanked him
for all that he mended,
and the class that he started
was quite well attended!

And as for Bilgewater Bob,
he made Squinty-eyed Jack his first mate.
It was known far and wide
on the seas when he died,
that he wore his sweater-vest
with great pride!

The End

Over and Under

Your underwear aren't under
if they're all that you have on,
and an overcoat's not over
if your underwear is gone.

Haiku

What a funny word.
It sounds like someone sneezing.
Please, use a hanky.

A Serious Poem

I wanted to write
a serious poem,
so I locked myself up
in my bedroom at home.
I thought and I thunk and
I thinked and I thank,
and I wrote and I rhymed
'til my armpits both stank!

I finally produced one
of which I was proud,
well proud, I confess,
'til I read it aloud.
It sounded so bad
that in all likelihood,
I'll be giving up serious poeming
for good!